<u>Dedicated To:</u>
Natalie
November 15, 1996

<u>Written By:</u> Abigail Gartland

Hello, my name is St. Albert the Great!

I was born in German in 1200.

had a strong love for Jesus my whole life.

When I was young, I learned lots of important things at my school.

I studied different writers and the faith.

When I was a young man, I became a priest. Then I became a bishop!

I was a well known teacher of the faith.

One of my students was St. Thomas Aquinas!

During my life, I spent lots of time writing.

My favorite things to write about were friendship, love and philosophy. This mean thinking about the world.

I also studied science and medicine.

Do you want to be more like me?

You can celebrate my feast day with me on November 15th.

I am the patron saint of scientists!

I pray for you every day of your life.

St. Albert, pray for us!

yright:

art: © PentoolPixie © LimeandKiwiDesigns
sed purchased: 1/10/2024

About the Author

Abigail Gartland

I love the saints and I love my faith. The idea for sharing the stories of the saints with little ones came when my dear friend were expecting their first baby. I wanted t create something as unique and special as our friendship. Each book is dedicated to very special people and groups who have enriched my faith in different ways. I am blessed to write these stories and appreciate the unending support of my family and friends. When I am not writing am a middle school teacher. I hope you enjoy these stories. I pray for each and every person who opens one of my books to learn more about the saints.

Abbie

www.ingramcontent.com/pod-product-compliance
Lightning Source LLC
LaVergne TN
LVHW051044070526
838201LV00067B/4908